Caring for Tropical Fish

Beginner's Guide to Setting Up and Maintaining a Thriving Aquarium of Tropical Fish

By Kenton Swinson

© **Copyright 2023 - All rights reserved.**

The content contained within this book may not be reproduced, duplicated or transmitted without direct written permission from the author or the publisher.

Under no circumstances will any blame or legal responsibility be held against the publisher or author for any damages, reparation, or monetary loss due to the information contained within this book. Either directly or indirectly.

Legal Notice:

This book is copyright protected. This book is only for personal use. You cannot amend, distribute, sell, use, quote or paraphrase any part, or the content within this book, without the consent of the author or publisher.

Disclaimer Notice:

Please note the information contained within this document is for educational and entertainment purposes only. All effort has been executed to present accurate, up to date and reliable, complete information. No warranties of any kind are declared or implied. Readers acknowledge that the author is not engaging in the rendering of legal, financial, medical or professional advice. The content within this book has been derived from various sources. Please consult a licensed professional before attempting any techniques outlined in this book.

By reading this document, the reader agrees that under no

circumstances is the author responsible for any losses, direct or indirect, which are incurred as a result of the use of information contained within this document, including, but not limited to, —errors, omissions, or inaccuracies.

Contents

Introduction 1

How to Take Care of Fish and Sustain Them 2

Advice For Looking After the Fish and the Aquarium 4

Caring For African Carp 7

Caring for Angelfish 9

Dealing With Dangerous Fish 12

Creating the Right Environment For the Fish 15

Taking Care of the Hemigrammus Species of Fish 18

Taking Care of Catfish 22

Maintaining the Aquarium 24

Looking After Goldfish 27

Creating a Safe Environment 30

Taking Care of Tropical Freshwater Fish 33

Relating to the Fish 35

Taking Care of Barbs 38

Dealing With Bizarre Fish 40

Dealing With Brachydanio 43

Caring for Callichthyidae 45

Caring After Carp 48

Taking Care of Catfish 51

Dealing With the Fancier Fish 54

Ensuring the Proper Filtration 57

Things You Should Be Checking Regularly 60

Caring For Coldwater Fish 62

Caring For Gasteropelecidae 64
Looking After the Harlequin Fish 66
All About Filters 69
Killifish and Loach Fish 72
Caring For Leopard Filefish 75
Taking Care of Marine Fish 78
Caring For Mollies and Guppy Fish 81
Taking Care of the Nannostomus Fish 83
Taking Care of the Pomacentridae Fish 86
Caring for Puntius Fish 89
Caring For the Silver Dollar Species 92
Taking Care of Tetra Fish 95
Starter Kits 98
Tools For Maintaining Your Aquarium 100
Maintaining Aquarium Water in Order 102
Water Treatment 104

Thank you for buying this book and I hope that you will find it useful. If you will want to share your thoughts on this book, you can do so by leaving a review on the Amazon page, it helps me out a lot.

Introduction

As people become more aware of the pollution in nature, they are turning to aquariums to bring the beauty of nature into their homes. The advancements in technology have made it easier than ever to set up and maintain an aquarium, with features such as switches and controls. This has led to a growing need for information on fish care and aquarium maintenance.

This guide contains all the necessary information on fish types, aquarium types, care, filters, and more to help aquarists properly maintain their fish tanks. With this guide, you can do less and have more success with your aquarium.

How to Take Care of Fish and Sustain Them

Freshwater fish are a good choice for beginners as they can adapt to most aquarium types. They tend to be more relaxed and informal compared to saltwater fish. Some examples of freshwater fish include the common goldfish, Reedfish, Banjo Catfish, and Bumblebee Goby. Saltwater fish, on the other hand, include the Powder Blue Surgeonfish, Clown Surgeonfish, Gold Rim Surgeonfish, and Leopard Filefish.

Once you have decided on the type of fish, you will need to choose the appropriate tank. Saltwater fish generally prefer Reef Tanks, while goldfish do well in slow, flowing dwellings. It's important to place the aquarium on sturdy flooring and avoid placing it near windows, heaters, and doors.

Filtration systems are necessary to keep the aquarium free of harmful chemicals and algae. The filters come in various types, such as chemical, carbon, mechanical, and biological. Water treatments are also important to remove anything the filtration systems miss.

Goldfish are adaptable fish that can live in tropical environments, but they need oxygen and a balanced water temperature. Reedfish, on the other hand, require a water temperature set between 73-79 degrees Fahrenheit and well-planted tanks. Checking manuals provided by pet shops can help you learn more about fish compatibility and care.

Advice For Looking After the Fish and the Aquarium

Aquariums have become popular green ecosystems in homes worldwide, as people strive to preserve what is left of nature due to air and water pollution. Aquariums today are designed by technological personnel to resemble real water environments, but they are still substitutes for nature.

You can purchase tanks that allow you to adjust the water level and vary the intensity of the lights. On and off switches with automatic timers can also help you control the lighting and water in your tank. Maintaining tanks has become easier than ever with the use of filtration systems that purify the water and keep it balanced and free from pollutants. Electrical procedures can help you maintain optimum water values, and automated devices make it easy to manage food and dosage. You can purchase tanks in various shapes and sizes, including resistant water tanks, and stock them with a variety of plants and fish. Aquariums not only bring nature into your home, but they can also help you relax after a stressful day. When cleaning your tank, make sure the non-toxic sealants are watertight, and avoid using sealants that are less or more than 1 mm or 1/16 inches. Larger tanks should have at least 20 gallons of water. To position your tank, place it on a sturdy stand that can support its weight.

The water and tank capacity can be calculated by multiplying the length, width, height, and water capacity of the aquarium. Make sure the floor beneath the stand can hold the weight of the tank and avoid placing it near windows, doors, or heaters. To equip your tank, you will need a sturdy stand, tank, lighting system, heater, thermostat, and a sufficient filtration system. Decorations like stones, roots, and substrates can enhance the aesthetics of your aquarium. Water conditioners are ideal for neutralizing chemicals like chlorine. You will also need a bucket and net to maintain the tank. Filtration systems include chemical, biological, and mechanical filters, with internal, external, and under-gravel variants.

External filters are the most efficient, but under-gravel filters can be combined with internal or external filters to achieve good results. After setting up your tank, consider adding African Carps to your aquatic environment.

Caring For African Carp

The African Tooth Carp, belonging to the Genus Aphyosemion, is a popular carp species among aquarists. However, they are not suitable for communal tanks as they are territorial and aggressive towards their own kind. Male carps are especially aggressive and must only be housed with females. As they have a short lifespan, it is recommended to keep them in separate aquariums. These fish are beautiful but prefer a shady environment with floating plants. The tank should have purified overcooked peat at the bottom and the water condition should be moderately hard or slightly acidic. Some carps prefer alkaline water, and adding 1 teaspoon of table salt to a gallon of water can help achieve this condition.

There are three types of breeders: surface, midlevel, and bottom breeders. The first two types require floating or fine leaf plants, respectively, for egg attachment. The third type requires peat situated at the bottom of the tank. Bottom breeders also need sterile peat and floating plants. Water temperature should remain at 25 degrees Fahrenheit, except for peaty waters where it should be set at 65 degrees Fahrenheit. To avoid fatality, you must refresh the tank with soft water, while shaking the peat. Bottom breeders can be kept in smaller tanks and require removal of parent fish after egg delivery. Water siphoning is also necessary, but you must avoid siphoning the eggs and peat. Temperature should remain constant for a couple of weeks before adjusting to 65 degrees Fahrenheit.

For beginners, it is best to avoid this species and choose other fish kin to the Carp family that are less demanding. The Zebra Danio or Brachydanio Rerio is a great option for starters. These fish are less demanding and prefer peaceful waters. They are shaped like cylinders and have attractive colors, including gold, silver, blue, and black. Angelfish is another aquarium species that may interest aquarists.

Caring for Angelfish

Angelfish, a large breed of the Pterophyllum spp. Cichlidae family, is a popular choice for aquarium fish enthusiasts. These fish have deep-shaped bodies with anal and dorsal fins that vary in color. They have curved eyes offset by small pouting lips and can have blue sheens and black spots, making them highly desirable. Angelfish prefer to live in water temperatures of 72 degrees Fahrenheit, except during breeding when the temperature needs to be between 77 and 86 degrees Fahrenheit. They prefer wild, natural environments with flourishing vegetation and require sufficient covering to feel secure. They also have bones in their throat area, which can cause noise during breeding.

Another popular fish for aquariums is the Harlequin fish, also known as Rasbora Heteromorpha, which belongs to the Cyprinidae family. This cute fish has a thickset, deep shape with a silver-gray tone and shimmering sheens.

It also has a light underside with a patch of purple-black and/or blue on its body and grows up to 1 ¾ inches in size. Harlequin fish prefer warm waters with a tank temperature between 75 and 77 degrees Fahrenheit, increasing to 82 degrees Fahrenheit during breeding. They require a pH balance between 5.3 and 5.7 and prefer hard water conditions with a rate of 1.5 to 2.5. They require sufficient swimming room, slighting filtered peat water, and subdued lights.

Scat, from the Scatophagus Argus group and family Scatophagidae, is another interesting fish for aquariums. This fish has a golden brown tone with brownish spots and is shaped like a hexagonal. It grows up to 11 ¾ inches in size and prefers brackish, seawater, or freshwater to dwell in. Scat fish require a neutral pH balance and strong alkalinity, as well as hard water. A ratio of 2 gallons of water to 3 or 4 teaspoons of salt is recommended. They prefer good lighting and a substrate area with sand. Scat fish eat plants but prefer tougher plant groups. They require a sturdy filter and frequent water changes. Scat fish have a peaceful nature and swim in a wobbling motion, preferring to dwell with compatible fish.

For beginners in fish care and aquariums, it is best to avoid difficult and dangerous fish such as piranhas until they gain more experience. Angelfish, Harlequin fish, and Scat fish are great options for starting out.

Dealing With Dangerous Fish

Characidae is a type of fish belonging to the Ostariophysi species, known for their small connective tissues or adipose fins, jaws with teeth, and Weberian bony structures linking to their bladders and inner ears.

Characidae fish are mostly found in South and Central America, but can also be found in some areas of Central Africa. They can be categorized as either carnivorous, herbivorous or omnivorous, depending on their feeding habits. While omnivorous Characidae eat both vegetables and animals, carnivorous species mostly consume meat.

The herbivorous Characidae species can be harmful to aquariums, as they can nibble on plants and damage the tank. It is important to note that Characidae fish may attack and gnaw at smaller fish like Angelfish and Fighters, and can cause significant damage to the aquarium. Piranhas, which are similar in appearance and behavior to Characidae, are notorious for their sharp teeth and strong jaws, and can attack in groups. Therefore, it is recommended that beginners in fish care and aquariums stay away from these species. Characidae fish mainly feed on meat, such as worms.

They prefer to live in soft swampy waters, as it provides a conducive environment for breeding. However, Characidae can also eat their own eggs or young, so it is important to have the right skills and knowledge before attempting to breed them. The Serrasalmus Rhombeus, commonly known as Spotted Piranha or White Piranha, is a type of fish that grows up to 10 inches in size and is native to the Amazon Basins and South America. They have a deep pressed body with silvery or olive green colors, and strong teeth used to devour other creatures.

Piranhas are not recommended for beginner aquarium keepers, and they should not be placed with passive fish. Piranhas feed mainly on lean meats and other fish, and are carnivorous in nature. While they are not picky with water conditions, they should not be kept in the same aquarium as other piranhas as they can eat each other.

Creating the Right Environment For the Fish

With over 20,000 different types of fish, it can be overwhelming to learn about every single one. However, there are some basic principles of tank management that can help you take care of your fish. Unlike animals on land, fish do not have fur or coats to protect them, which is why water temperature is crucial. If the water is too hot, there won't be enough oxygen, and if it's too cold, it can negatively affect the health of your fish. Your aquarium should come with a manual or instruction brochure, so make sure to read it to know the exact temperature and gravity required for your fish. For example, goldfish should be kept at around 75 degrees Fahrenheit, while tropical fish should be between 75-85 degrees Fahrenheit.

Measuring water pH is also essential for fish care. It is measured on a scale of sourness, which varies depending on the type of fish. Saltwater fish require a pH of 7.8-8.3, while freshwater fish should be between 6.8-7.2. Monitoring pH levels is important, as higher levels can produce more ammonia, which can be harmful to your fish. You can purchase buffers and test kits to maintain the right pH balance. Gravity is also measured in water, as well as oxygen, which is necessary for the survival of all living beings. You can increase oxygen levels in your aquarium by using pumps or air supply, and keeping the water cool can also help.

For saltwater fish, maintaining the right environment can be a bit more complicated. Marine creatures live in constantly changing environments, so it's important to keep the water stable. If you've purchased a larger aquarium, it's easier to maintain a stable environment for your fish. The Damsel's is a beginner's saltwater fish that requires little attention and is easier to maintain than other saltwater fish. However, it's important to note that Damsel's are aggressive and don't mate well with other fish. Learning about the Hemigrammus can also be helpful in maintaining saltwater fish aquariums.

Taking Care of the Hemigrammus Species of Fish

Hemigrammus is a diverse genus of tetra fish, including the Erythrozonus, Rhodostomus, Flammeus, and many others. The Flammeus belongs to the Hyphessobrycon group. Erythrozonus, also known as the Glowlight Tetra, was once wrongly classified as Hyphessobrycon Gracilis. It comes from British Guiana and reaches a size of 1 ¾ inches, boasting a glowing ruby red body. However, unfavorable water conditions can alter its colors. The Erythrozonus is a friendly fish that cohabitates well with other non-aggressive fish and can eat most foods. It is a small and brightly colored member of the Characin family, thriving in tropical tanks.

Water Conditions: The tank temperature should be maintained at 78-80 degrees Fahrenheit, with a dark background and thick plants.

The Hemigrammus Erythrozonus breeds best in peaty waters or acriflavine methods. For more information on breeding this fish, consult with pet shop experts, who will provide helpful brochures. The fish lays up to 400 eggs that hatch in one day.

The Hemigrammus Rhodostomus, also known as the Rummy/Red Nosed Tetra, comes from the Amazon and grows to be 2 inches in size. It boasts a brilliantly red colored snout and has a peaceful nature. This hardy fish will eat all sorts of food.

The water should be kept at 78 degrees Fahrenheit and slightly acidic or reasonably soft. Breeding this fish is challenging, so consider other fish species if you lack breeding skills.

The Hyphessobrycon Flammeus, commonly referred to as Flame Tetra or Tetra Von Rio, originates from the neighboring areas of Rio de

Janeiro. It grows to only 1 ½ inches in size, making it shorter than other species, and has a shimmering red lower body.

This hardy fish is an excellent choice for an aquarium and has minimal water condition requirements. It breeds well, laying up to 200 eggs that hatch in one day.

Another species related to Hemigrammus Erythrozonus is the Hyphessobrycon Pulchripinnis, also known as the Lemon Tetra. This smaller fish grows to be around 1 ¾ inches in size, featuring a distinctive pale lemony color and a brilliant red patch above its eye.

The Lemon Tetra is an ideal social tank fish that feeds on most foods and is peaceful in nature. It prefers softer water conditions, with a temperature of 80 degrees and slightly acidic water. Male Lemon fish have a better color choice. However, breeding this fish can be challenging, so try peaty waters.

Paracheirodon innesi is a Brazilian Neon Tetra that grows to be around 1 ¼ inches in size and is one of the most popular tank fishes sold on the market. It has a greenish-blue and deep red body combined, is a hardy fish that can take care of itself among smaller and larger fish, and generally rests at the bottom of an aquarium. The fish eats all types of food, but breeding is also difficult.

Taking Care of Catfish

Catfish are a popular aquarium fish as they are great at cleaning algae and debris from tanks. However, some species are more difficult to maintain than others. Among the popular choices are Black Spotted Corydoras, which are known for their small size and silver body with black spots. They are also peaceful and won't harm other fish. Another popular choice is the Peppered Corydoras, which has an olive-brown body with small black marks and is commonly found with the Corydoras aeneus group. They enjoy the same food and water conditions as other Corydoras Catfish species and are also good at removing debris and algae from tanks.

Another type of catfish is the Leopard Corydoras, which has a silver-gray body with dark spotted stripes and grows to be 2 ½ inches in size. They are peaceful and handle communal tank water well, and prefer the same water conditions and feeding as other Corydoras Catfish species.

The Loricariidae Catfish, also known as the armor catfish or sucking fish, is a popular choice among aquarists as they are great at eating algae and removing debris from tanks. They come from the northern and central parts of South America and have bony plates protecting most of their body. Their mouth is located beneath a flat head with wide rounded lips. While they won't rid the tank of complete contaminants, they do significantly cut back on the need for tank cleaning.

Maintaining the Aquarium

Once you've purchased your aquarium, it's important to learn how to properly care for your fish. Before buying anything, it's a good idea to research the market to gain an understanding of fish care and tank maintenance. Here are some helpful tips:

Heaters are necessary for maintaining tropical fish. Make sure to purchase a heater and filters that fit your aquarium without taking up too much space. If you have a small tank, you may need to purchase smaller filters and a heater, or consider upgrading to a larger tank.

In addition to the tank, you'll want to purchase gravel, plants, ornaments, food, test kits, water treatment, and more. Gravel helps maintain natural resources, ornaments provide a lively decor, and plants make fish feel at home. Test kits and water treatment are necessary for monitoring and maintaining the health of your tank.

After rinsing your gravel to remove grime, dirt, and germs, add half the water needed to fill the tank, then add your ornaments and plants. Once everything is in the tank, add the rest of the water, and follow the tank's manual for filling instructions. Next, add your heater and filtration systems, and then the water treatment. Allow the tank to settle for a couple of weeks before adding fish.

When adding fish to your tank, start with passive fish, and gradually add more fish over time. Damsels are recommended for saltwater tanks, but be aware that aggressive fish can eat passive fish. For freshwater tanks, consider starter fish like White Cloud Mountain Minnows or Danios, and passive fish like Bristle Nose, Otocinclus, Plecostomas, Marble, or Veiltail.

If you want both saltwater and freshwater fish, it's best to purchase two separate tanks to avoid any complications. Remember to always monitor the temperature, chemicals, and bacterial levels of your tank, and to follow instructions carefully for proper care and maintenance of your fish.

Looking After Goldfish

The majority of aquarium fish accidents are caused by owners' lack of knowledge in proper fish care. If you plan to keep fish at home, it is crucial that you learn about the types of fish and how to take care of them. Patience is also required. Goldfish are a popular fish that require adequate care and attention. If you have any concerns while caring for your goldfish or other fish, call a local pet store and seek assistance. Books on fish care are also available at your local library to help you care for your fish.

It's essential to maintain the tank and provide enough space for your goldfish to swim. While you may have seen goldfish kept in small containers or bowls on TV shows, this is a bad idea. Goldfish require room to breathe, and oxygen comes from the surface of the aquarium, just like any other living creature. Ensure that the aquarium offers sufficient space based on the length, depth of the tank, and the number of inches of fish. For every inch of goldfish, it is recommended that you have at least 30 square inches of surface space. Goldfish grow in size, so add a few extra squares to ensure that the fish have enough oxygen.

If you haven't purchased goldfish or an aquarium yet, ask the service representatives at your local pet store what type of tank would be best for goldfish. You need to know how many fish you plan to house in the tank. Additionally, there are several goldfish varieties on the market, so having a basic idea of what type of fish you want can help the service representative provide you with aquarium information. If you haven't bought an aquarium or goldfish yet and have an idea of what you want, it's recommended that you research. Fish are living creatures, and it's the owner's responsibility to preserve their lives. Research can help you become knowledgeable about what you need to do and the maintenance required for your aquarium and goldfish. If you plan to have plants or other types of fish in your aquarium, make sure you have a basic understanding of each plant and fish as well.

Fish require high-quality water with a few exceptions. Tap water is okay to use, but it tends to build up pollutants. You can ask your local pet store for advice to ensure that tap water in your area is suitable for fish maintenance. It's recommended that you run the tap water for at least five minutes before using it to fill the tank when using tap water to refresh fish water. Running the water for five minutes will remove or dissipate chemicals from the water. You can also let the water sit overnight after running it for five minutes to remove additional chemicals.

Water contains chlorine, copper, metals, and other contaminants. All times, keep goldfish water pure and free of chemicals. Filters, vacuums, gravel, floss, etc., are all available to help you maintain clean fish water. Ammonia builds up in aquariums, so it's essential to understand filtration as well. Your primary targets are chemical, biological, and mechanical filters.

Creating a Safe Environment

There are over 20,000 types of fish, which makes it impossible to cover all aspects of fish care and aquarium maintenance in one article. However, there are some basic concepts and care instructions that can help you get started. One of the most important things to consider when caring for fish is the toxins that can be present in both the water and the fish themselves. Aquariums are designed to provide a habitat for fish and other aquatic animals, and the water in these containers must be maintained to ensure the survival of these creatures.

The temperature of the water is crucial, as fish cannot control their body temperature like other animals. Using dehumidifiers or humidifiers can help maintain a balanced temperature in the air, which will affect the water temperature.

You can also use fish gauges to monitor the temperature in the water. Fish in tanks or aquariums are more susceptible to bacteria and toxins because they do not have natural defenses like land animals. Thus, it is essential to provide high-quality water to the fish. Both saltwater and freshwater fish require proper care, and you need to understand the differences and how to maintain the water supply for each species.

Toxins can come from a variety of sources, including fish waste, chemicals added to the water, and pollutants in the water supply. You can use a test kit to monitor toxin levels in the water and use filters and pre-treatment water to balance your aquarium. To remove toxins from the water, you can expose the tank to air, combine gas and liquids to activate carbons, or use products like water purifiers to eliminate contaminants.

If you find metals or copper in the water, you may need to use spring water or purified water to remove toxins. Additionally, you can use hepa products that connect to your tap water and eliminate metal, copper, and other contaminants.

Taking Care of Tropical Freshwater Fish

The Holacanthus Trimaculatus category includes the Three-Spot Angelfish, which is a family member of the Trimaculatus group. These tropical fish have a beautiful golden-yellow body with dark blue lips. The Three-Spot Angelfish is found in the West Pacific and Indian oceans and grows up to 10 inches in size. This species got its name from the two upper dark patches on its body, as well as the colors at the edges of its gill-covered flaps and on top of its head. The fish prefers to live in water conditions similar to that of the butterfly fish and feeds on plants, larvae, and small creatures.

The Pajama Cardinal Fish, which belongs to the Apogonidae family, originates from the China Seas and Indo-Australian seas. It prefers to live in shaded areas with a water temperature set at 75 to 80 degrees Fahrenheit and a pH8 balance. This highly predatorily fish feeds on smaller fish, crustaceans, and large planktons. The fish has distinctive thread-like dorsal fins and a big mouth with large eyes. It prefers to dwell in peaceful areas and compatible housing with school fish.

The Yellow-Tailed Anemone fish is a member of the Amphiprion Clarkii group and belongs to the Pomacentridae family. These fish usually reside near the bottom of tanks and require compatible kin and anemone for their social life. They come from the Eastern areas of Africa and Sumatra and grow up to 5 inches in size. They are yellow, white, dark brown, and black colored fish.

Frogfish belong to the Antennariuus Spp. Group and the Anennaridae family. These fish reside in warm seawater and have territorial behavior patterns. They require compatible company, preferably larger kin with peaceful natures. It is important to note that these fish are known to capture and eat fish larger than their own size.

Relating to the Fish

When it comes to Aquarium and Fish Care, it's important to consider the type of fish you have, whether they are saltwater or freshwater fish, and whether they are tropical or coldwater fish. In this article, we'll explore a few different types of fish to help you get started.

Pantodontidae includes only a few different types of fish, including the freshwater flying fish and the butterfly fish. These fish are native to West Africa and typically grow to about 4 inches in size. Butterfly fish have a flat body shape that tapers at the snout and is made up of small bold patterns. They are part of the Chaetodontidae family, which is also known as Pantodontidae in Latin. These fish are relatively passive and should be kept with their own species or size.

Pantodontidae fish prefer to dine on smaller fish such as minnows and insects. They can also be trained to eat meaty dishes or even worms with a long stick.

Pantodontidae fish prefer temperate soft water with a temperature of around 80 degrees Fahrenheit. Butterfly fish also prefer waters with thicket plants that rise above water.

Mormyridae fish come from South and Central African Pools and are part of the electric fish category. These fish have a body ratio weight and brain weight that compares to humans. They have a good sense of humor and are curious and easy to teach. If you decide to purchase Mormyridae fish, make sure to maintain their diet to avoid food decline due to feeble myogenic organs.

This breed of fish is commonly known as the trunkfish or elephant trunkfish. They come from Central Congo and grow to be about 4 inches in size. These fish have silvery-brownish bodies with dark bands and dull tubercle, which differs from the G. Petersi species.

Gnathonemus Petersi, also known as the elephant nosed fish, grow to about 4 inches in size and come from Cameroon and Congo. These fish have elongated chins that are sideways and squeezed against the body. They are colored black or darker brown and have two white stripes on their body. These fish are passive and can be kept in communal aquariums. They eat freshwater fleas and enjoy Tubifex, a common fish worm. They prefer to hide, so keep the water temperature at 80 degrees and the tank filled with plenty of plants. Barbs are a more appealing choice of fish to keep with Gnathonemus Petersi.

Remember to consider the specific needs of each type of fish you have to ensure they receive proper care and attention.

Taking Care of Barbs

When it comes to freshwater fish, barbs are one of the easiest breeds to maintain and breed. However, larger barbs should be kept with fish of similar size to prevent trouble in communal tanks and damage to plants.

The Black Ruby and Purple Head Barbs are breeds from Ceylon that grow to be around 2 ½ inches in size and live well in communal tanks. The female barbs have yellow-gray figures with dark stripes, while the males are black or brownish-black with vermilion red frontals. This breed is not finicky and will feast on all types of food.

The Tiger Barb and Sumatra, on the other hand, are of the Capoeta Tetrazona species and come from Borneo and Sumatra. They grow to be around 2 inches in size and set off communal tanks with their reddish-yellow figures with black stripes. Their temperament is changeable, with some claiming they are bullies while others say they have a calming nature. They require similar water conditions to other barbs and should be fed a hearty diet. Female Tiger and Sumatra fish are plump compared to their male counterparts, and fry tend to have bladder problems and fin rot.

Cherry Barbs or Capoeta Titteya fish are another breed that originates from Ceylon and grow to be around 2 inches in size. They make great communal fish and have dark top to bottom black stripes. Male Cherry Barbs have darker colors and can change colors when bred.

In conclusion, Harlequins are a great fish to consider if you are just getting started with fish care and aquariums, and there are many other unique fish breeds to explore as well.

Dealing With Bizarre Fish

Sailfin Mollies, a type of Poeciliida fish, are characterized by their long dorsal fins that are raised high. These fish are originally from the river estuary and coastal zones of Yucatan and are available for purchase in pet stores due to their desirable blue-green metallic marks and orange-black fins. Female Sailfin Mollies are distinguished by their blue-gray fins. These fish prefer warm water environments with a temperature range of 73 to 82 degrees Fahrenheit, a water density similar to the pH balance, and salt added to the water. They also prefer substrate areas, well-lit environments, and the presence of plants and detritus on the bottom of the tank. Sailfin Mollies are social and enjoy live bait and vegetable matter occasionally.

African Lungfish, belonging to the protopteridae family, are snake-like creatures commonly found in the Zaire River Basin. These fish have dorsal, anal, and caudal fins that form at the tail area, and pectorals and pelvic fins that resemble threads. They prefer quiet environments with running waters and fresh dry mud at all times. African Lungfish adapt well to varying water conditions and require a lower volume of oxygen. They feed on fish, snails, worms, and mussels and can also be fed with beef heart, lean meats, and stripped fish. African Lungfish care for their young and spawns and require compatible tankmates due to their lower oxygen needs.

Serrasalmus Rhombeus, also known as Spotted Piranhas and White Piranhas, are part of the piranha group and are captured from the Amazon Basins and South America waters. Piranhas can grow up to 10 inches in size in the wild, but only up to 6 inches in captivity. These fish have deep pressed bodies with silvery or olive green colors and razor-sharp teeth that they use to tear and devour prey. Piranhas are aggressive fish and should not be kept in tanks with passive fish. They are known to dine on large and small fish and can even threaten humans with their lower jaw lines. Brachydanio is another fish group that can be considered.

Dealing With Brachydanio

Brachydanio Albolineatus, Rerio, Nigrofasciatus, and more are all popular species of aquarium fish, with the Albolineatus also known as the Gold Danio or Pearl Danio. These fish come from Sumatra or India and grow up to 2 inches in length, with a sleek, pearlescent body that shimmers in various colors. The Albolineatus is a calm and peaceful fish that thrives in community tanks with plants and darker gravel. It is also intelligent and prefers similar water conditions and food to the Rerio breed, which is also a popular choice for breeding due to its ease of care. The Nigrofasciatus, or Spotted Danio, is another similar species that grows to around 1.5 inches in size and requires the same conditions for breeding as the Rerio.

The Giant Danio, or Danio Aequipinnatus, is a larger species that grows up to 4 inches in length and is found in India and Ceylon. This fish has a silver body with a blue and yellow stripe and a voracious appetite, making it suitable for larger communal tanks. The Aequipinnatus is not overly demanding when it comes to water conditions and can thrive in neutral or moderately hard water, as well as larger tanks. These fish lay semi-adhesive eggs that hatch in around 3 days, and prefer to spawn in tanks with pebbles at the bottom. For other fish to consider, check out the Callichthyidae group.

Caring for Callichthyidae

The Mail and Armored Catfish are a popular choice among fish enthusiasts, originating from Trinidad and South America. These catfish have bony plates covering their body, which provide protection from larger fish. The fins are movable and surrounded by adipose, with the dorsal fins located near the backbone. Two sets of barbel can be found at the base of their mouth.

Another popular catfish group is the Genus Corydoras, known for their hardy nature and amusing features. They are great for cleaning up pollutants in the tank. If you plan on breeding mail or armored catfish, a separate tank is necessary. It's important to create a suitable environment for them, including fine gravel and minimal plant volume. The water temperature should be around 72 degrees Fahrenheit and not overheated, with moderate alkalinity, hardness, or neutral conditions. When it's time for spawning, a separate tank with up to 15 gallons of water is recommended, with the water temperature reduced to around 62 degrees Fahrenheit. The fish will lay eggs up to 400 in number, which will hatch in a few days. Methylene blue is added to the tank to prevent rotting and provide a peaceful environment for the fry. Micro worms and saltwater shrimp are great foods for the fry.

Bronze Corydoras, also known as Corydoras Aeneus, come from Venezuela and Trinidad waters and grow up to 2 ½ inches in size. Although they are not a popular choice for tank water, they make good communal tank fish and won't harm other fish. The Bronze Cory enjoys Tubifex and white worms, as well as dried foods. It's important to maintain a neutral water condition with moderate volume and avoid saltwater.

In summary, whether you choose Mail and Armored Catfish or Genus Corydoras, it's crucial to provide a suitable environment for them and maintain proper water conditions to ensure their health and longevity.

Caring After Carp

The Asiatic Tooth Carps are fascinating little fish found in ditches, streams, and ponds. They belong to the Genera Aplochelilus and Oryzias and require water temperatures between 70 to 80 degrees Fahrenheit. These fish have a preference for living near the surface and do not like hard alkaline water. In the wild, the Tooth Carps feed on insects and mosquito larvae, but in captivity, they can eat dried food as well.

Tooth Carps do best in smaller or medium-sized tanks with 10 gallons of water or less, and prefer moderately hard, acidic water with peaty substrates, fine leaf plants, and lime-free gravel. Breeding Tooth Carps Tooth Carps spawn quickly and will lay a small number of eggs daily over a period of three weeks. Although they won't harm their eggs, they will consume their own fry. To save the fry, you can either remove the parents or transfer the eggs to a different tank with lots of plants. Sorting through the fry by size can also prevent cannibalism.

The Dwarf Green Panchax, also known as Panchax Parvus, is closely related to the Tooth Carps and comes from the Aplocheilus blocki group. These fish are native to India and Ceylon and mature at 1 ¾ inches in size. Dwarf Green Panchax is suitable for aquariums as they are mild-tempered fish and have a green-yellow shaded body with rows of yellow and red marks. They feed on both dried and live foods.

During breeding, the water temperature should be set at 78 degrees Fahrenheit. The fry generally hatch within two weeks. It is advisable to breed Dwarf Green Panchax with two males and multiple females.

The Geisha Girl Medaka, also known as the Ricefish or Japanese Medaka, belongs to the Oryzias latipes family and is native to Japan. These fish grow up to ½ inch in size and have a unique breeding pattern. The Geisha Girl

Medaka is adaptable to soft to moderately acidic water, and if you choose the latter, adding a leveled teaspoon of salt to 3 gallons of water is recommended. They prefer water temperatures set at 78 degrees Fahrenheit but can survive in water temperatures ranging from 75 to 80 degrees Fahrenheit. Female Geisha Girl Medaka can be identified by their rounded fins and plumper body, and are shorter than their male counterparts.

Overall, these fish make excellent aquarium pets and offer a fascinating and enjoyable experience for enthusiasts.

Taking Care of Catfish

Catfish are a diverse group of fish that include the Siluridae, which are actually descendants of the Catfish family. The European catfish is related to the Asiatic group and includes the naked skinned fish. However, the Siluridae group is one of the less popular aquarium fish due to their translucent layers of skin. On the other hand, the Glass Catfish, which belong to the Kryptopterus Bicirrhis group, are more desirable. These fish grow up to 3 ½ inches in size and have glass-like bodies with extended anal fins and barbel on their upper jaw line. Glass Catfish are best kept with their own kind and feed on living foods.

The Mockokidae is another group of helpful catfish that originate from African waters. They feed off biochemicals, including decomposed macrobiotic bodies and dead fish, and help maintain tank photosynthetic organisms like algae. Catfish are unique in that they are composed of bones rather than cartilages and have distinctive fins that differ from flesh-like fins. They also lack scales but have sensitive whiskers that can detect touch, smell, and taste.

The upside-down Catfish in the Synodontis Nigriventris category comes from Belgian Congo and is shaped like the Corydoras group. This species is a communal tank habitat fish that feeds off photosynthetic organisms and live bait extracted from leaves beneath the surface. The Electric Catfish, on the other hand, is from the Malapterurus Electricus group and can grow up to 10 feet in natural waters but only two feet in aquarium water. These fish have electrical organs and can produce a disturbing shock, making it necessary to keep them in isolated confinement.

In terms of feeding, the Electric Catfish is an insatiable nighttime diner that eats meats, worms, and other fish smaller than its size. It does not have a preferred water condition as long as it has water and plenty of food. Overall, catfish are an interesting and diverse group of fish that offer a unique addition to any aquarium.

Dealing With the Fancier Fish

With so many different types of fish in both saltwater and freshwater environments, it can be overwhelming to know where to start when it comes to fish care and aquariums. It's important to learn the basics of starter fish, which are usually passive, peaceful, and easy to maintain. One of these starter fish is the Discus Fish, also known as Symphysodon aequifasciata and s. discus fish. Despite its intimidating name, the Discus Fish is a brilliantly colored tropical fish that lives in freshwater with water temperatures set between 82-88 degrees Fahrenheit and a pH level between 6.0-6.5.

Discus fish are slow feeders and tend to reside by themselves, but can live in communal tank water with smaller and peaceful fish such as the Corydoras catfish, cardinal tetras, and Rasbora. It's important to review the health of Discus fish before purchasing, as they can be difficult to save if they become ill. Discus fish are finicky eaters and enjoy live bait, frozen foods, beef heart shredded, and Tubifex, although the latter should be washed carefully before feeding to avoid disease.

If you're looking for a fancier fish, Bettas, Gouramies, and Fighting Siamese Fish are popular options that spread out in the waters of Asia and live well in aquariums. These fish are commonly exploited in Thailand and enjoy battling, with a variety of colors to choose from including red, blue, bicolor, and even albino.

Fish can be categorized into saltwater (marine) fish or freshwater (non-marine) fish, with freshwater fish including tropical and coldwater fish. Tropical fish are more desirable for starters in fish care and aquarium keeping, with a wide array available at pet stores and online.

It's important to know the type of water the fish comes from in order to choose the best-suited water conditions. Most pet stores provide instructions for fish care, which should be read carefully, and don't forget about filtration systems.

Ensuring the Proper Filtration

Effective filtration systems are crucial for maintaining a healthy aquarium and keeping your fish happy. The purpose of filtration is to remove chemicals and pollutants from the water, which can be achieved through various methods such as mechanical, chemical, and biological filtration.

Mechanical filtration physically traps suspended particles of grime and dirt that are too large to pass through the fibres or pores of a filtration medium. Polyester fibres are commonly used in mechanical filtration systems and come in a variety of forms including pads, fluffs, and pressed fibers. Foam sponges can also be used to block particles and suspend water.

Chemical filtration breaks down pollutants on a molecular level, with activated charcoal being one of the most popular choices. Carbon filtration is another widely used filter that removes contaminants and delivers clear water. It's recommended to combine carbon filtration with mechanical filtration, although many modern mechanical filtration systems already integrate carbon filters into their design.

Biological filtration is the most crucial filtering system for aquarium and fish care. It removes both natural and unnatural particles from the water that are unseen by the human eye. This process involves fish, bacteria, and biochemicals that work together to remove and replace microscopic pores and contaminants in a bio-medium environment. Biofiltration systems remove unwanted nitrates, ammonia, bacteria, and nitrates, but replace them with a healthy volume of nitrites.

There are different types of filtration systems including internal, external, and under-gravel systems. The under-gravel system is less popular, but it can work in combination with the internal and external filtration systems. External filtration systems are more commonly used because they combine mechanical, chemical, and biological filtration systems effectively.

Filtration is essential in aquarium and fish care, as unfriendly waters can affect the fish's oxygen intake and lead to their death. Therefore, it's important to understand the different filtration systems available and choose the right one for your aquarium. Consult with pet stores or seek additional help online to make the best decision for your fish and their environment.

Things You Should Be Checking Regularly

Taking care of fish is important, and it depends on the type of fish you have, whether it's saltwater or freshwater. You also need to consider the type of aquarium you have for your fish. Monitoring your fish daily is crucial for maintaining their health. Knowing your fish and their behavior patterns can help you spot any changes in their health or behavior.

Feeding your fish according to their needs is also important, and you should remove any buildup of algae regularly. To maintain the water quality in your aquarium, using filters and removing chlorine buildup is necessary. Adding calcium and iodine salt is also recommended for saltwater fish. You should also remove 10-15% of the aquarium water every week and refill it with pure water. Tap water can contain harmful chemicals, so it's important to consult with your local pet shop to ensure the water is safe for your fish. Using chemical, biological, and mechanical filtration systems can also help maintain water quality.

When changing the fish water, removing debris from the gravel is essential. Testing kits are also important to monitor nitrite, ammonia, chlorine, metal, copper, and nitrate levels, as well as pH levels. Alkalinity buildup should also be checked monthly. Filters should be checked every two weeks, and replaced when necessary. Keeping records of fish care and aquarium maintenance is also recommended. For more information, check online resources.

Caring For Coldwater Fish

Caring for coldwater fish can be a great starting point for beginners in the world of fish care. These fish are adaptable and can thrive in different water temperatures, but it is still essential to ensure that the aquarium is kept clean to maintain oxygen supply. To keep the water clean, adding filtration systems and plants to the tank is a great idea. Plants can produce oxygen and help remove waste, while filters can help perform similar actions synthetically. When purchasing an aquarium, it is important to consider the size, stands, lights, hoods, and thermometers.

Choosing the right aquarium size is crucial, with a minimum liter capacity of 45 recommended and sizes above 130 being the best. Long, wide, and large tanks are easier to maintain and allow you to add a variety of fish without overcrowding. To choose a stand, you need to consider the weight of your aquarium, stability, and whether it attaches to walls for additional security. Lighting is essential for plants to feed and grow, so consider fluorescent lights that provide an adequate amount of heat and intensity. Hoods are also important to prevent fish from jumping out and to keep out unwanted particles and critters.

A thermometer is necessary to measure temperature, and there are many types available in the market. It is recommended to ask your local pet shop for assistance in choosing the right thermometer for your aquarium. Besides tanks, hoods, lights, and plants, you also need to purchase gravel, filters, heaters, and appropriate food for your fish. When selecting fish, the Gasteropelecidae group has some fascinating options to consider.

Caring For Gasteropelecidae

Maintaining fish tanks can be made easier with the help of advanced technology. Today's tanks have features that allow you to adjust water temperature and light intensity. Electronic devices can control the quality of water and automate feeding and fertilization. Water-resistant tanks are available in various sizes and shapes and can accommodate a range of fish and plant species. However, it is important to understand the preferences of the 22,000 fish species before selecting the right tank and fish for your home. Different fish species require specific water conditions and types of food. Certain breeds, such as the Piranhas, are considered dangerous and require special care.

Flying fish, such as the Gasteropelecidae or Hatchetfishes, are known for their ability to escape tanks by flapping their chest fins. The Carnegiella Marthae or Blackwing Hatchetfish is a popular species that prefers peaceful waters and soft water conditions.

Another Hatchetfish species is the Gasteropelecus Levis or Silver Hatchetfish, which is known for its silver color and blue-blackish stripes.

The Cyprinidae family includes Carp-like fish and Carps, which are freshwater fish found in North America, Asia, Europe, and Africa. The Indian Mahseer Carp or Barbus tor is the largest Carp breed, growing up to 8 feet. Minnows, which are freshwater baitfish, are also part of this family. Harlequin fish require special attention in terms of fish care.

Looking After the Harlequin Fish

The Harlequin fish, also known as the Red Rasbora fish, belongs to the Rasbora Heteromorpha groups that originate from Thailand, Sumatra, and the Malayas. These smaller breeds of fish are popular among aquarium keepers because of their colorful figures. With blue-black shades that set off their rosy pink and violet forms, the Harlequin fish is shaped like a wedge. They are easily trained and do well in communal tanks, although they are so beautifully formed and colored that they can produce natural effects in a sole tank. Harlequin fish eat all kinds of food and prefer water conditions such as soft water, sensibly acidic waters, and peaty waters. Breeding Harlequin fish is not easy, but it is possible if they pair in well-conditioned waters or peaty waters with a pH balance of pH-6, pH-2, or hard water at 40-ppm. These fish typically lay fewer than one hundred eggs, which turn into fry in one day.

The Cobitidae family is another group of fish that helps keep tanks clean by gnawing at algae. They are similar to Carps, as they have teeth, and have four barbel located in their upper jaw. These fish also belong to the European freshwater Cyprinids family, which includes minnows and Carps. Spiny Loach is the family of Cobitidae, and this fish composes of bifid spines located beneath the eyes that are erect from their folded, flat position when challenged by predators. These fish often surface to seek oxygen and prefer to live in murky, mud-spattered waters. The Loach fish include the Acanthophthalmus Semicinctus family that comes from the east parts of India and grows up to 3 ½ inches in size. The Half Band Coolie, as it is popularly called, has a body shaped like a snake and covers yellow and black marks. Kuhlii fish tend to fall into the Salmon category, as they may have pink bellies, as well as yellow and black marks, and are similar to the sub-species of the Coolie family. Coolie fish are communal tank fish and have a peaceful nature. They tend to eat Tubifex and algae, making them a good cleaning system. These fish tend to do well in moderate or neutral waters and prefer a water temperature of 78 degrees Fahrenheit.

Lastly, there are the Clown Loach, Tiger Botia, Siluridae, and so on. The internet offers a wide assortment of information related to freshwater fish, including tropical fish, Coldwater fish, sea, or saltwater fish. Tank maintenance depends on the type of fish, and today's tanks have switches that enable you to change the water temperature and dim or intensify tank lights. Water is purified via a filtration system, and the quality of water is controlled by electronic devices. Automated features enable you to distribute food and fertilize dosage. Water-resistant tanks come in a variety of shapes and sizes and use electrical advanced solutions to maintain safety. Tanks also enable you to stock plants and fish of all species, and the lights can be adjusted to accommodate most fish types. However, fish are different in many ways, and understanding their preferences is key to keeping them healthy and happy in your aquarium.

All About Filters

To maintain a healthy fish tank environment, it is crucial to use filters that can eliminate toxins from both natural and man-made sources. The two main types of filters are biological filters and chemical/mechanical filters. Biological filters work by removing nitrogen from water through the process of denitrification. By using bacteria to convert ammonia compounds into nitrates, nitrogen becomes available for fish. Nitrogen is an odorless, colorless gas that chemically changes into natural resources. On the other hand, mechanical filters remove solid waste and particles from the water using foam filtration cartridges, gravel, and floss. Chemical filters remove ammonia and soften water using activated carbons and absorbents, and water purification systems can minimize chemical buildup.

Various types of aquarium filters are available, including corner filtration, outside powered filters, under-gravel filtration, foam, canisters, and flow-through filtration. Corner filtration involves using air to create a vacuum that extracts water into the filter. Floss filtration can be added to activate carbons to assist in filtering the tank water, which creates a biochemical reaction that slows the growth of bacteria. Outside powered filters use electrical pumps to extract large amounts of water through filters that pass over filtered floss and carbons to provide adequate water supply. Under-gravel filtration works as a vacuum that extracts water from the gravel, providing biological and mechanical aids without using chemicals. Foam filtration attaches to air supplies to supply ventilation and biochemical reactions that filter the growth of bacteria. Canisters are filters that combine mechanical, biological, and chemical filtrations using a pump. Flow-through filtration provides continual drainage solutions and water supplies, but the water must be conditioned.

In terms of the types of fish suitable for aquariums, the Harlequin fish or Rasbora Heteromorpha is a small, peaceful, and colorful species that grows up to 1 ¾ inches in size.

Coolie fish or Acanthophthalmus Semicinctus are shaped like a snake, with yellow and black marks covering their body. They eat Tubifex and algae and do not place a high demand on water conditions. Killifish are also popular but may be harder to find. It is important to change the filters regularly, as dirt buildup decreases their efficiency.

Killifish and Loach Fish

Fish, just like humans, require certain things to survive, such as oxygen, food, water, cleanliness, and companionship. Water is the primary source of survival for fish. Freshwater fish cannot tolerate large amounts of saltwater, but some can tolerate a small amount of salt. On the other hand, saltwater fish require saltwater to survive, as they come from oceans, seas, and related waters worldwide. Freshwater fish, however, come from ponds, streams, lakes, and rivers, and some popular fish include the Killifish and Loach fish.

Loach fish come in various types, including the Cobitidae family, which primarily consists of nocturnal catfish. They tend to live at the bottom of the water and use their barbels to sift through gravel. The Kuli Loach, with its snake-like or worm-shaped body, is a popular choice for aquariums. This fish is shy and prefers hiding in the back corners of the tank or in caves. It is peaceful and can live in communal tanks with other fish of its kind. The Kuli Loach likes to eat Tubifex and prefers neutral or slightly acidic water conditions without bright lights.

The Botias, including the Tiger and Clown Fish, are some of the easiest Loach fish to care for and prefer moderate hard or alkaline water conditions. They do not thrive in acidic waters and require a water temperature of no higher than 75 degrees Fahrenheit. Botias make excellent neighbors in communal tanks.

Killifish, which come from the Cyprinodontidae family, have the brightest colors of all freshwater and saltwater fishes. They are ideal for beginners and can live in communal tanks. The fish are found in African Sub-Saharan waters and can live in small tanks with water conditions set between 70 and 85 degrees Fahrenheit. They prefer peat filtered waters, but can tolerate slightly acidic, soft, or hard waters. Killifish enjoy a variety of frozen and dried foods.

Leopard Balistidae is another fish worth learning about. They are a type of triggerfish that have a unique appearance with spots like those of a leopard. They can grow up to 20 inches in size and require a minimum tank size of 125 gallons. The fish are known for their aggression and should be kept alone or with other aggressive fish. They require a varied diet of meaty foods and vegetable matter.

In summary, fish require certain things to survive, including oxygen, food, water, cleanliness, companionship, and appropriate water conditions. Different types of fish have different requirements, and it is important to do research before adding them to your aquarium.

Caring For Leopard Filefish

The Leopard Filefish is a fascinating fish from the Balistidae family that caught my attention. This fish may not be the prettiest fish in the ocean, but it has a friendly biological nature and can coexist with other aquarium fish. The fish can be found in the Pacific, Atlantic, and Indian Oceans, as well as the Red Sea. The Gold Rim fish is slightly more attractive than the Leopard Filefish but has a similar diet of omnivorous foods and sting sea anemones.

Environmental conditions for the Leopard Filefish include a water temperature between 75 and 82 degrees Fahrenheit, a water density of 1.023, and a pH balance around eight. The fish needs sandy-bottomed tanks with substrate and well-lit areas, as well as sheltered structures in vertical nature. The fish also needs hiding spaces and can be fed omnivorous foods and sting sea anemones.

The Frogfish is another group of ugly fish that belongs to the Antennariidae family and is part of the Antennarius spp. group. The fish has a unique appearance, resembling a combination of a fish and frog. The fish is clumsy and squat with a fishing rod, growths on its thick skin, and no known sexual preference. The fish can camouflage amongst other fish and grows up to 5 to 8 inches in size.

Environmental conditions for the Frogfish depend on the type of environment it prefers, and advice from a supplier is necessary. The fish is territorial and needs a surplus of rocks in the aquarium for hiding spaces to hunt its food. Frogfish can overpower larger fish groups, so careful consideration is necessary for which fish to house with this critter. The fish can be fed strips of meat and/or fish.

Other interesting marine fish include the Boxfish or Trunkfish and the Pufferfish, which derive from the Ostracion spp. The Boxfish has a yellow frame with block spots, and its eyes are rimmed in darker yellow with blackish eyes. The fish requires a water temperature of 75 to 86 degrees Fahrenheit and a water density of 1.018 to 1.030, with good lighting and a sandy bottom. The fish is sociable and has interesting eye behaviors, but some of the Trunkfish, Loach, or Boxfish have an unsociable nature and are vicious.

Taking Care of Marine Fish

The world of marine fish is diverse and fascinating, with many breeds to choose from. Two popular breeds are the Acanthurus leucosternon and Acanthurus lineadae. The Acanthurus leucosternon, also known as the Powder Blue Surgeonfish, has a distinctive black mask on its face, a sky blue body with yellow stripes, and grows up to almost a foot in size. This fish feeds on algae, but also eats smaller creatures and particular shrimps, as well as dried foods and vegetables. They prefer water temperatures between 77 and 84 degrees Fahrenheit, a pH balance of 8.2 to 9.4, and a water density of 1.020. These fish are energetic and prefer to roam on their own, making them better suited for tanks without other fish.

The Acanthurus lineadae, or Clown Surgeonfish, is also from the Acanthuridae family and is found in various areas of the Pacific Indian Oceans. This fish has electric blue, violet, or gray-blue colors with yellow-brownish pinstripes and a narrow caudal fin. They grow up to 8 inches in size and prefer water temperatures between 75 and 82 degrees Fahrenheit, a pH balance level over eight, and water density at 1.023. These fish have a nervous nature and do not adapt easily to aquarium foods, preferring zooplanktons as their main diet. They also prefer luxury tank furnishings and hiding corners, and should be kept with their own kin due to their anti-social side.

The Gold Rim Surgeonfish, or Acanthurus Glaucopareius, has a brown tinted shade with blue/orange fins and white-striped cheeks. These fish grow up to almost 14 inches in size and prefer water temperatures between 75 and 77 degrees Fahrenheit, a pH level of eight, and water density at 1.027. They prefer sand and stone substrate environments, good lighting, and a variety of foods. These fish are known for their active swimming behavior and are a great addition to any tank.

Other interesting marine fish include the Molly and Guppy, which are found in the marine category. The world of marine fish is truly diverse and there are many breeds to explore and enjoy.

Caring For Mollies and Guppy Fish

Poecilia spp. and the Poeciliidae family are home to the beloved Mollies, a favorite among tank fish enthusiasts. They share similarities with the swordtail fish, but instead of a swordtail, they have a larger dorsal fin. With a variety of shapes and sizes, Mollies can grow up to 4 to 4 ¾ inches in size, while males grow to a maximum of 3 1/3 or 4 inches. These sociable livebearers prefer a wide range of environments and will thrive in estuaries. Mollies can handle temperatures between 72 and 82 degrees Fahrenheit and prefer hard water with a pH level of 7-8. Furnishing, lighting, and plants are important for their overall well-being. Mollies are omnivorous and enjoy feeding on vegetables, including spinach and algae. Their lively biological nature is suited for constant water flow and they breed successfully in communal tanks with large schools.

The Guppy fish, also known as Poecilia reticulata, comes from the Poeciliidae family and is found in Guyana, Venezuela, Brazil, Trinidad, and Barbados. They prefer still, flowing waters with temperatures ranging from 68-75 degrees Fahrenheit and a pH level of 7-8. Guppies can survive in hard water and prefer illuminated tanks with plenty of vegetation and plants. They will eat all sorts of food and have a loose school nature, always on the go.

Modern aquariums have become ecosystems with advanced technology, including circuits, plugs, filters, and air supply. They allow for easy adjustment of water temperatures and light intensity with mechanical timers. Most tanks can accommodate nearly all fish available on the market, but it's important to keep fish that prefer to live with their own kind together. Freshwater and saltwater fish have different requirements. Freshwater fish include Tropical and Coldwater fish.

Taking Care of the Nannostomus Fish

If you're interested in setting up an aquarium, it's important to do your research and learn about the different types of fish available. Understanding the needs and preferences of each species can help you provide the best possible care for your fish and maintain a healthy tank.

Thankfully, modern aquariums come equipped with a range of electronic devices and controls that make it easier than ever to keep your tank in top condition. However, it's important to remember that different fish require different water conditions, such as hard or soft water, acidic or alkaline water, and so on.

One species to consider is the Nannostomus, which includes several different types of pencilfish. The Nannostomus Eques, or Brown-Tailed Pencilfish, hails from the Amazon and grows to about 2 inches in size. This peaceful fish prefers water temperatures between 78-80 degrees Fahrenheit and tends to spawn on broadleaf plants. The Nannostomus Marginatus, or Dwarf Pencilfish, is even smaller at only 1.25 inches, but boasts striking black stripes with red accents on its fins. This introverted fish prefers to live with smaller fish in peaceful communal tanks.

Another member of the Nannostomus family is the Unifasciatus, or Tail-eyed Pencilfish, which is one of the most colorful breeds on the market. This friendly species grows to around 2 inches and prefers similar water conditions as its Nannostomus relatives. Finally, the Beckford's Pencilfish, also known as the Golden Pencilfish, is a peaceful and hardy species that grows to 1.75 inches. This species is suitable for communal tanks and comes from the Guiana and Amazon Basin.

By learning more about the different types of fish available and their unique needs and preferences, you can choose the best species for your aquarium and ensure that your fish thrive in their new home.

Taking Care of the Pomacentridae Fish

The Pomacentridae family includes various types of fish, such as the Amphiprion Rubrocinctus and the Amphiprion Ocellaris. Amphiprion Rubrocinctus, commonly known as the Clown Anemone Fish, is native to the Australian, Japanese, and Indo-Pacific waters. These fish have bright orange bodies with black edges and white perpendicular bars. The Clown Anemone Fish is a high maintenance fish that prefers water temperatures between 77 and 82 degrees Fahrenheit, pH balance at eight and no higher than 8.5, and a water density of 1.023.

These fish tend to closely associate with chemicals and mechanisms of two distinctive organisms, and they demand capable dwelling. Clown fish should be kept in the same tank as other fish of their kind, and avoid putting sea anemones, including the giant anemones, in the tank, as these pose risks to the Clown fish.

Another fish in the Pomacentridae family is the Red-Gridled Anemone. This species is similar to the Clown fish, preferring luxury housing with plenty of furnishing and quality lighting. The Red-Gridled fish has a deep body with bright orange colors and a head that is pale orange. These fish prefer water temperatures between 75 degrees and 86 degrees Fahrenheit, a water density of around 1.020 or 1.023, and a pH balance of 8.3 and no higher than 8.6.

The Pomacentridae family also includes the Orange Fin Anemone and the Black Back Anemone. The Orange fin fish swim in the tropical Indo-Pacific Ocean and have light yellowish-orange colors with vertical white bars. On the other hand, the Black Back fish, which roam the Andaman Seas, has glowing orange contrasted colors, black patches highlight the orange body, and yellowish toned fins. The Black Back fish is considered prettier than the Orange Fin, but loses its color during maturity. Overall, knowing the specific needs and characteristics of different fish species is essential for proper fish care and maintaining a healthy aquarium.

Caring for Puntius Fish

If you want to have fish as pets, it is important to educate yourself on fish care and how to maintain aquariums properly. Fish are living creatures that require food, clean water, oxygen, attention, and a healthy environment. If you are not prepared to take care of these needs, it is best to avoid getting fish as pets altogether. Fortunately, modern aquariums are designed to be self-sufficient, with switches and controls to regulate lighting, filters, food, dosages, and more. Test kits are also available to help you monitor the chemical levels in the water. To help you select the right fish breed, let's take a look at a few types of fish.

Barbs are a popular group of fish that come in a wide variety of colors and designs. They are generally active and easy to feed, making them a great choice for beginners. Barbs are also tolerant of different water conditions. However, larger barbs can be destructive and may cause trouble in tanks. It is important to separate smaller and larger barbs in communal tanks. If you want to breed fish, barbs are a good choice, and their eggs should be placed on pebbles or plants. The Puntius Conchonius, also known as the Red Barb or Rosy Barb, is a popular breed that comes from India. They grow up to 2 1/2 inches in size and have silver bodies with deep rosy red covers. These fish are calm and quiet, but also energetic and boisterous. They prefer moderate hard water with neutral alkalinity and a temperature of 78 degrees Fahrenheit.

Another breed of barb is the Puntius Nigrofasciatus, also known as the Purple Head Barbs or the Black Ruby. They come from Ceylon and grow to about 2 1/2 inches in size. The male and female counterparts differ in color, with the females presenting dark stripes over a yellowish-gray figure. These fish are easy to breed and can tolerate most water conditions and foods.

If you're looking for a different type of fish, the Silver Dollar is another option. These fish are part of the Metynnis family and are known for their large, silver scales that resemble coins. They grow up to 6 inches in size and prefer a pH level between 6.0 and 7.5, with a temperature between 75 and 82 degrees Fahrenheit. Silver Dollars are peaceful fish and can be kept with other species that have similar water requirements.

Remember, fish require a lot of attention and care to thrive in captivity. Make sure you educate yourself on the specific needs of the fish you choose and provide them with a suitable environment to ensure their health and well-being.

Caring For the Silver Dollar Species

Silver Dollar, scientifically known as Metynnis Lippincottianus, is a popular fish species that originates from the Amazon Basin and can grow up to 5 inches in size. This fish has an oval-shaped body and is peaceful in nature, preferring to live harmoniously with other fish of the same species in a large tank. However, Silver Dollar fish have a tendency to destroy plants, so feeding them adequately is crucial to prevent them from destroying the plants. They are known to feed on lettuce, sprouts, spinach, and meaty dishes. This fish species likes moderate soft water conditions with slightly acidic water, and they breed quickly and produce hundreds of eggs.

Metynnis Hypsauchen or Shreitmueller is another fish species from the Amazon Basin that grows up to 6 inches in size and has similar characteristics to the Silver Dollar fish. However, they lay thousands of eggs in one hatching, so preparing for a larger army is necessary, and the hatchlings must have a water temperature of 82 degrees.

Gymnocorymbus Ternetzi or the Black Tetra fish is also known as Petticoat and Blackamoor fish, and it comes from Bolivia, Argentina, and Brazil. This fish grows up to 2 inches in size and has fan-like fins that are often black. They are ideal for a tank, but they have a habit of nibbling at other fish's fins. They can feed on dry foods and a variety of other food items, and the water temperature should remain at 68 degrees or 70 degrees Fahrenheit. Gymnocorymbus Ternetzi fish lay hundreds of eggs, which hatch in a day, and the hatchlings require infusoria food.

Pristella Maxillaris, also known as X-ray fish, Goldfinch, or Pristella, is a small fish species that originates from northern South America and grows up to 1.5 inches in size. This fish has a transparent body and is passive in nature, making it suitable for community tanks. Pristella Maxillaris feeds on all kinds of food and requires water temperature set between 72 degrees and

78 degrees Fahrenheit. They lay up to 500 eggs and are relatively easy to breed.

Other fish species available at pet stores include Hemigrammus Erythrozonus, Hyphessobrycon Flammeus, and Paracheirodon innesi. The Hyphessobrycon Pulchripinnis is another species available. However, starting fish owners should avoid Piranhas and Characin species since they are carnivores and may eat other fish and fleshy dishes. These fish species are better left to experienced fish owners.

Taking Care of Tetra Fish

Tetra fish are a popular choice for freshwater tanks due to their vibrant colors and tropical origins. They belong to the Characidae family, but there are many different varieties available, including the Anostomidae family. The Anostomus-Anostomus, also known as the Striped Anostomus or Headstander, is a South American fish that can grow up to 6 inches in size. It has a cylindrical body with a long, pointed snout and gold and black stripes with red dots. This fish is not recommended for communal tanks, but it can live with larger fish and prefers a water temperature of 78 degrees Fahrenheit.

The Pearl Headstander, or Chilodus Punctatus, is another type of Headstander fish that originates from North and South America. It grows up to 3 ½ inches and has a grayish-green body with rows of brown specks. This peaceful fish can be kept in communal tanks and prefers slightly acidic water with a temperature of around 80 degrees Fahrenheit. It feeds on a variety of foods, but should be given green vegetables like spinach and lettuce.

The Lebiasinidae family is similar to the Characins, but with a lower jawline that lacks teeth. This South American fish has an elongated body and is also known as the Pencilfish. The Nannostomus Beckfordi, or Golden Pencilfish, is a species in this family that originated from British Guiana and the Amazon Basin. It grows up to 1 ¾ inches and has a golden-brown body with black stripes and red or gold patterns. This peaceful fish is ideal for communal tanks and prefers soft, slightly acidic water with a temperature of 80 degrees Fahrenheit.

In summary, tetra fish are a popular choice for freshwater tanks due to their colorful appearance and tropical origins. There are many different varieties available, including the Anostomidae and Lebiasinidae families. These fish have different characteristics and preferences, so it's important to do your research before adding them to your tank.

Starter Kits

When you're looking to set up your own fish tank, it's important to consider the nitrogen cycle and the chemicals that are produced by fish. Starter kits are available online that include additives such as ammonia, which is necessary for the tank. Goldfish are great starter fish for coldwater tanks, and they produce an adequate supply of ammonia. Plants can also help purify the tank by absorbing chemicals and providing oxygen. They also break down ammonia and filter out bacteria in the water. Use test kits to check the level of ammonia in the water and avoid overfeeding the fish.

Make sure that you have a secure stand for your tank and avoid placing it near windows, doors, or heaters. Once your tank is set up, add pre-washed gravel and start adding ornaments and plants. Use marine-based plants and fill the tank halfway with pre-treated water. Prime the filters and install them along with heaters after setting up the tank properly. If you chose a fish other than goldfish to ammonize the tank, wait a few weeks before adding fish. If you choose goldfish, you can add them to the tank to start the process.

To prepare the fish for the tank water, allow them to float at the top of the aquarium while still in their bag. You will also need lights and a hood to fit over the top of your aquarium to regulate the tank lights and keep out critters. Overall, setting up a fish tank requires some preparation and patience, but the end result is a beautiful and rewarding addition to your home.

Tools For Maintaining Your Aquarium

To maintain an aquarium, you will need several tools such as siphons, scrapers, nets, buckets, water treatments, filters, gravel, ornaments, air pumps, and plants. Filters are essential to keep out unwanted chemicals and debris from the water. You can choose from biological, chemical, or mechanical filters and opt for under-gravel, internal, or external filters. Although external filters are better, they can be more expensive than the other options. You can also combine under-gravel filters with either internal or external filters.

When choosing gravel, it's best to get it from local pet stores, where the staff can advise you on the best options. Pre-washed gravel is also a popular choice, but if you buy non-washed gravel, you will need to boil, cleanse, and prepare it before using it. Similarly, when choosing ornaments, you should seek advice from pet store representatives or read the labels.

When selecting plants, choose ones that are suitable for your aquarium's needs and won't grow higher than your tank. Marine water plants or fish plants are good options. For air pumps, it's best to ask the professionals since there are various options available, and the pumps must accommodate the size of your aquarium.

In addition to pumps, tools, plants, filters, etc., you will also need test kits to monitor the quality of water and avoid overconsumption of nitrates, ammonia, nitrites, etc. Water treatments are also necessary to maintain water quality, and chlorine treatments are ideal for removing chloramines and chlorine from tap water, which can be harmful to fish. If you're a beginner, look up information about starter kits and beginner fish, including saltwater and freshwater fish. Tropical fish, in particular, can be fascinating, so do your research and enjoy the process of setting up and maintaining your aquarium.

Maintaining Aquarium Water in Order

Nowadays, aquariums have become more advanced and can be self-sufficient to a certain extent. It's important to check water conditions since the quality of water varies depending on the region, and different fish species and plants have different water requirements. For example, Tetras thrive in soft water, while Cichlids prefer harder water with dissolved salt.

To avoid hardening the water, it's best to avoid adding limestone, especially if you're using it as rocks or gravel. You can test the water's pH level using a test kit, which you can purchase online or at your local pet store. A pH reading below seven indicates acidic water, while a reading above seven indicates alkaline water. The ideal pH level is seven, which is neutral. If the pH level is too high or too low, it can negatively affect your fish and plants.

When setting up your aquarium, it's important to use water conditioners to remove any chemicals, such as chlorine, from tap water. If you're using a heater, it's best to keep the volume low and use a heaterstat to regulate the heat. Plants and fish from tropical regions are more adaptable to higher water or room temperatures, but it's generally not recommended to place an aquarium in a living room since the warmer temperature can agitate the fish.

In summary, maintaining a healthy aquarium requires testing water conditions regularly, providing the right environment for your fish and plants, and using the appropriate tools and equipment. With proper care, your fish and plants can live long and healthy lives in your aquarium.

Water Treatment

Fish require a specific pH level in their water, typically ranging from 6.5 to 7.5. There are various types of water, such as saltwater, alkalinity, hardness, and soft water. Alkalinity water can be measured using buffers, which help to regulate the pH balance of the water and prevent it from dropping. If necessary, buffers can be added to adjust the alkalinity levels. Hard water contains high levels of minerals, which can be harmful to fish. Soft water lacks dissolved minerals, while water softened by machines may not supply a variety of minerals. To combat this issue, water treatments are commonly used by aquarium owners to treat tap water before adding it to the tank.

Water treatments can include NH_3, NO_2, and NO_3, which represent chemical formulas for ammonia, nitrites, and nitrates respectively. Test kits are recommended for beginners to measure ammonia, nitrites, nitrates, chlorine, and other chemicals in the water. Fish naturally produce ammonia through waste, which turns into nitrites, so testing should be done during the tank cycle. It's important to treat tap water before adding it to the tank, as chlorine and chloramines can be harmful to fish.

There is a myth that salt should be added to all fish tanks, but in reality, it's not necessary for all types of fish. Some tropical fish may benefit from added salt to relieve stress. Water treatments often include dechlorinators, which purify the water by removing chloramines, although they can discharge ammonias. It's important to know what is in your tap water before choosing a water treatment. Tap water can contain chemicals like chloramines, copper, chlorine, metal, phosphates, and TCE. To purify tap water, you can let it run for five minutes or let it stand overnight. Sodium-based thiosulphate dechlorinators can be used if tap water only contains chlorine, but if it contains additional chemicals, it's best to speak with a local pet store operator for advice on the best water treatments.

I hope that you enjoyed reading through this book and that you have found it useful. If you want to share your thoughts on this book, you can do so by leaving a review on the Amazon page. Have a great rest of the day.

Printed in Great Britain
by Amazon